D1795335

About the author

Ray Chidell (MA Cantab) works in the field of UK taxation as a consultant and professional author. He has had several major books published, written for businesses, accountants and other professionals.

Ray was brought up as an Anglican but joined the Catholic church at Easter 1987. This booklet is the first he has written on a topic outside his area of professional interest.

Ray lives in Chester with his wife Maryla. They have three sons and Ray has seven god-children. This booklet is written for all of them.

Acknowledgements

I am grateful to many people for their encouragement and intelligent criticism. At the risk of omitting many others, my particular thanks go to the Franciscan friars in Chester (especially Fr Gordon and Fr Keith) to Sylvia and Jim Turner, to Sister Seraphim and, especially, to my wife Maryla.

Feedback and further copies

The author invites comments on the text, whether positive or not. They can be sent by e-mail to raychidell@gmail.com or by post to the address opposite.

Further copies of the booklet will be supplied on request.

See also www.believewithreason.org.uk.

For

Adam, Michael, Philip

and

William, Julian, David, Gabriel,
Nicola, Pierre, Victoria

Table of Contents

~ Introduction ~

I was struck by a radio debate between an Oxford university professor, who was an ardent atheist, and two senior religious figures of different faiths. The professor was taking the line that in the twenty-first century the very idea of the existence of God was a self-evident nonsense, something not even worthy of discussion.

There are plenty of reasons why a person might question the existence of the Christian God: the difficulty of reconciling an all-powerful and all-loving God with the suffering we hear about each day; the fact that religions, between them, can seem to do so much more harm than good, or at least that so much harm is done in the name of religion; the fact that the Bible seems to be far from literally true in many areas; the fact that Christians have been slow to accept that the earth is not 4,000 or so years old, and that the sun does not revolve around the earth; perhaps even the idea of eternity.

But many reasons for denying the existence of God are far less convincing. There is a prevalent view, for example, that science has somehow explained all the mysteries of the universe, and that religion – invented by our ignorant forebears to explain such mysteries – is therefore not "needed" any more. The reality is that while many phenomena have been explained, many others have either not been explained at all or have been the subject of explanations that are no more than theoretical.

Most (but not all) Christians would now accept that the Old Testament accounts of creation are not to be taken literally. Darwinian evolution has been explained and brought up to date by such writers as Richard Dawkins (another atheist Oxford professor). But for many the theory of evolution still raises more questions than it answers; science does not, for example, have any satisfactory explanation of how matter is created out of nothing or how life is created out of no life.

Much of what Dawkins has to say about the *possibility* of natural selection is persuasive but other parts of his arguments leave at least some readers unconvinced.

There are also, of course, plenty of reasons why people prefer not to believe. Christianity (in common with the other big faiths) is seen as imposing a set of rules that can be uncomfortable or even offensive for those who have bought fully into twenty-first century western values. To give just one example, the Christian church, and particularly the Catholic church, is known to take a strong stance on such issues as abortion and euthanasia. It can therefore be *convenient* to take the view that the belief system is simply nonsense as all the difficult rules then fall away. Even the most ardent atheist, though, would admit that this is a poor basis for concluding that God does not exist.

But is there any sense in which it is difficult *not* to believe? That, really, is the theme of this booklet. For it seems to me that there are plenty of happenings, from 2,000 (and more) years ago to the present day, that need an explanation and that rationalists cannot explain.

Atheist scientists such as Dawkins do not claim to *prove* that there is no God. Dawkins, though, refers to the analogy put forward by Bertrand Russell of whether there is a teapot in orbit around Mars[1]. You cannot prove that there is no such teapot so technically you are always agnostic on the matter. Nevertheless, as the argument goes, any thinking person will conclude that the chances of there being such an orbiting teapot are so small that for all practical purposes it is safe to conclude that it is not there. By implication, no sane person can profess a religious belief in this great age of reason.

In reality, plenty of clever and deep-thinking individuals would still argue today that a creator is needed to explain the universe as we know it. Yet some atheists take the view that they are the only ones who still think about such issues and that all believers are merely suspending their natural judgmental faculties. This is unfair, arguably even a reversal of the reality: in my experience, many who claim a religious belief spend a great deal of time thinking about their faith, constantly grappling with the difficult issues and forever challenging themselves and one another. Many (but not all, of course) who reject all religious belief do so without giving it a fraction of such thought and evaluation.

It would be presumptuous for this short book to seek to offer *proof* of the existence of God, and that is not its intention. Its message is rather that – for those who do not believe but are open-minded – there are many reasons for honest doubt about their non-belief. I have three children and seven godchildren (two Anglican and five Catholic) who are growing up in a world where religious belief in general, and Christian belief in particular, is under attack from many sides. My aim is simply to challenge the atheists who claim to have all the answers, who say that religious belief is merely ridiculous, who claim that all believers have suspended their powers of reason, and who pretend that belief in God is as absurd as belief in that teapot orbiting Mars.

This is not a theological work; I am wholly unqualified to write such a book. In any case, there are plenty of others who have made a much more profound analysis of the relationship between faith and reason (see for example, the papal encyclical *Fides et Ratio*[2]) than I ever could.

Rather, this is a personal work, written primarily for those to whom it is dedicated. The questions raised are all considered on the lines that "there is good evidence that this happened and Christian belief appears to offer the only sensible explanation". In my capacity as father or godfather, I wish to share with those ten individuals something of my own thinking on a topic which – if it is anything at all – is ultimately more important than everything else.

Chapter 1

~ Did Jesus exist? ~

The Christian faith is centred on a man, Jesus Christ, who lived and died around 2,000 years ago. A good starting point is therefore to ask if there is evidence that such a person even existed as a historical figure; if there was no Jesus then there can be no Christianity.

The obvious place to begin is with the accounts kept by the early Christians themselves, eventually collected together to form the New Testament, the second (smaller) part of the bible. The New Testament begins with four "gospels" – a term that means, broadly, "good news" – which between them provide an account of the birth, life, teaching, death and resurrection of this man called Jesus. (The question of the resurrection is, of course, a major stumbling block for the non-believer, and will be discussed much more fully in later chapters.)

By way of background, there were many written accounts of the life of Jesus. The reasons for selecting the four that are now so familiar to Christians were complex and have been explored in great detail by many scholars. One intelligent and readable analysis, written early in the 20th century, may be found online[3]. Within about 150 years of Jesus' death, four such accounts had been selected as offering the definitive and official record of Jesus' life and teachings.

The four gospels were written from very different perspectives. The authors were all men (Matthew, Mark, Luke, John) but had widely varying backgrounds and approached their tasks in different ways. There is nevertheless considerable overlap between the accounts they give. This is especially true of the first three, whereas John presents his narrative with a more theological emphasis.

The differences of detail, content and approach are not of primary importance for present purposes. Many thousands of pages have been written on the subject and a good starting point for further research could be either Wikipedia, the free online encyclopaedia[4] or the Catholic encyclopaedia, which is again available online without charge[5].

Between them, the four gospels provide most of what we know about Jesus the man. We are told that he was Jewish, that his mother was Mary, and that he came from Nazareth but was born in Bethlehem. We are told that as an adult he became a teacher (or "Rabbi"), that he performed many healings of the sick and other miracles (discussed much more fully in later chapters), that he came into conflict with the official Jewish leaders of the time. And we are told that under the authority of the occupying Roman forces he was put to death by crucifixion.

In addition to the gospels, further evidence of Jesus' life is provided through the later books of the New Testament, in particular the *Acts of the Apostles* and the letters written by St Paul and others.

(The precise year of Jesus' birth and death are the subject of speculation but an in-depth analysis may be found in the Catholic online encyclopaedia[6]. The idea that Jesus was born in December, with snow and so on, is of course pure myth.)

We will come on later to the question of all the supernatural elements but how convincing is the assertion that there was a man by the name of Jesus who was born 2,000 years or so ago, who was a teacher and whose life formed the basis of the gospel records?

In fact, few people deny the existence of the historical figure. This amazing phenomenon that is Christianity, with the extraordinary effect that it has had on people's lives, must have had its roots somewhere; if Jesus the individual never lived then who created the whole myth, and why did that myth spread through the world?

It is entirely natural that most of the evidence concerning the existence of Jesus should come from the bible, but there are important snippets of external evidence too. Some 30 years after Jesus' death, Rome was devastated by a fire. The Roman historian Tacitus wrote about the events and explained how the emperor Nero blamed the Christians:

> "Nero fastened the guilt . . . on a class hated for their abominations, called Christians by the populace. Christus, from whom the name had its origin, suffered the extreme penalty during the reign of Tiberius at the hands of . . . Pontius Pilatus, and a most mischievous superstition, thus checked for the moment, again broke out not only in Judaea, the first source of the evil, but even in Rome"[7].

So here we have an independent account, clearly not biased in favour of the Christian viewpoint ("a most mischievous superstition" and even "the evil"), that there was a man called Christus who had been executed under Pontius Pilate, thus confirming both the existence of the man and his death at the hands of Pilate, two of the essential details of the gospel accounts. The text is significant for other reasons too and we will return to it later.

Pliny the Younger, who died early in the second century, was a Roman governor in Asia Minor. He wrote to the emperor Trajan for advice on how to handle the many people who stood accused of being Christians, a crime for which the penalty was death. Pliny wished to ensure that he was dealing correctly with the issue because of the great numbers of Christians of both sexes and of every age and class. The full text is available online[8] but the following is a key extract:

> "They ... used to meet on a certain fixed day before dawn, when they would sing a hymn in alternating verses

to Christ, as if to a god; and they bound themselves by a solemn oath, not to any evil actions, but instead to commit no fraud, theft or adultery, never to speak untruths, nor to deny a trust if called upon to deliver it up; after this they used to go their separate ways, and would then reassemble to take food – but food of an ordinary and innocent kind" [9].

Once more, the writing is revealing. Again, it was written by a man who had no sympathy for Christianity; he was, after all, seeking confirmation that he was right to execute the Christians. Yet it confirms that around the end of the first century AD there were large numbers of people who were meeting regularly and singing hymns to Christ "as if to a god".

There are other historical records, too, including Flavius Josephus, a Jewish man born around the year 37 AD whose history makes reference to the crucifixion of Jesus. The text also refers to followers of Jesus who were still proclaiming their faith several decades after Jesus' death. There are plenty of references to Flavius Josephus (a quarter of a million "hits" in Google at the end of June 2007, for anyone wishing to follow that lead). It must be acknowledged, though, that certain questions have been raised about the authenticity of the Josephus material.

It is also worth noting that both the other established monotheistic faiths, Islam and Judaism, believe that Jesus existed as a person. They disagree fundamentally with the Christian view of who he actually was (Islam honours him as a prophet whereas Judaism views him at best as an inspired teacher) but the three faiths are united in believing that Jesus existed and taught.

And finally, what do atheists say about the existence of Jesus as a human being? Arguably, it is not a fair question as atheism is simply the denial of belief in something supernatural, and there is therefore no "official" atheistic view on the matter. Nevertheless, a quick review of any number of atheist websites shows that the great majority of such sites acknowledge the existence of Jesus the man. They obviously view Jesus as nothing more than a man but most agree that he lived two thousand years ago in part of what we would now call the Middle East.

So Jews and Muslims, as well as most atheists, believe in the historic person of Jesus and there are near-contemporary texts that refer to his existence and to the early development of Christian beliefs. It is in a sense difficult to "prove" the existence of almost anybody from 2,000 years ago, except for a few individuals who were high-ranking officials or perhaps a few writers. But of all the debates that rage between different faiths, or between those with faith in a God and those without such faith, the question of whether Jesus actually existed is perhaps the least controversial of all.

Chapter 2

~ Jesus – worker of miracles? ~

It is one thing to believe in Jesus as a historical figure but quite another, of course, to believe that he was anything more than a normal human being.

Christians believe not only that he existed – as genuine a figure of history as, say, Julius Caesar – but that he is the "son of God", that in a mysterious way he *is* God. Indeed, Christians believe that he performed remarkable miracles, that he was tortured and put to death on a cross, but that he then "came back from the dead" and appeared to his followers. The concepts of miracles in general, and of rising from the dead in particular, are major obstacles for the non-believer; a standard atheist viewpoint would attribute the miracles to the power of the mind to overcome certain ailments and would say that the stories of the resurrection were either naïve or acts of deliberate deception. This chapter has a look at some of the miracles that are recounted in the bible.

The new testament is in fact overflowing with accounts of miracles performed by, or relating to, Jesus. For Christians, the greatest miracles would include:

- the Virgin Mary's conception of Jesus by the Holy Spirit (Matthew 1[10] or Luke 1);
- the resurrection of Jesus after his death and his ascension into heaven (all four gospels);
- the descent of the Holy Spirit onto the disciples some seven weeks after Jesus' death (Acts 2).

The non-believer would be particularly sceptical about the virgin birth, would by definition deny the resurrection and would view the story about the descent of the Holy Spirit as at best a delusion and at worst a fraud. So before considering these mega-miracles, what about some more down-to-earth, visible ones? Again, they are to be found in great numbers, including the following among many others:

- changing of water into wine at a wedding (John 2);
- mass healings of the sick (Matthew 4, 9, 15, 19; Mark 6; Luke 4, 6; Acts 5, 19, 28);
- the healing of a man who had been paralysed for 38 years (John 5);
- feeding 5000 people (or possibly that many men and an even greater number of women and children) (all four gospels);
- raising a man (John 11) and a girl (Matthew 9, Luke 8, Mark 5) from the dead.

Numerous websites, of course, contain details of the miracles, some with complete lists[11].

So what is the rational response in the twenty-first century to these accounts? We might view them in one of several ways:

- as deliberate illusions, equivalent to those performed by a modern entertainer or conman (the writer wrote an honest account of what he thought had taken place but he had been taken in);
- as the acts of an individual who thought he had mysterious powers but who was himself deluded (so, once more, the writer wrote an honest account of what he thought had taken place, but he did not realise that the performer of the miracles was mistaken);
- as pure lies or "myths" (no such events took place; the stories were invented by those who wrote them down, or by others who convinced the writer of their truth); or
- as the truth (these events took place and were honestly recorded).

Many might feel that they would "like to believe" that the last of these is true but that, after all, no such miracles happen today so reason forces us to opt for one of the other possibilities. We will return in a later chapter to the question of modern miracles but let's begin by considering the other options in turn.

Jesus as deliberate illusionist?

This is mentioned here as a possible view that people might take but a moment's thought shows that such a view is untenable.

There can be no illusion about healing huge numbers of sick people, about bringing certain individuals back from the dead, about calming a storm. Jesus was not in some sort of controlled one-hour TV show: he was out there dealing with real people with real problems and his public life spanned a period of about three years. In Jesus' time, modern medicine was of course unknown and there were many "healers" who claimed to perform miraculous cures. Perhaps some of them did indeed have certain healing powers but no records were kept of those healings and it seems fair to assume that they were on an altogether different scale.

The biggest illusion of all, of course, would be the resurrection of Jesus. If working alone, Jesus could never have created the illusion of his own resurrection from the dead: such a claim cannot hold water. His agonising death on the cross was a most public and, in human terms, final experience. He had been publicly flogged, a crown of thorns had been pressed onto his head, he had been nailed to the cross and his side had been pierced in such a way that blood and water came out.

One common conspiracy theory, though, is that Jesus was somehow drugged by his friends and that his death was faked. His accomplices then took him down from the cross and he simply recovered. But this is surely no more than a desperate claim by those who can find no more convincing explanation of the resurrection.

For a start, the whole question of Jesus' own motivation makes no sense. It is recorded (and indeed it would have been pretty obvious) that Jesus was on a collision course with the authorities, yet he headed for Jerusalem where the issues were all bound to come to a head. Jesus' death was clearly in fulfilment of an old testament prophecy (see Psalm 22, for just one example); he knew he was heading for trouble and he could have avoided it. There would have been no point going through the extreme torture and humiliation (not to mention the high risk of death) whilst gambling on successfully faking death.

And then there is the fact that the Romans were neither stupid nor inexperienced in the matter of crucifixion – they used it commonly and would have been wide awake to any possible abuses. Even if Jesus' death had been faked, a heavy stone was rolled across the entrance to the tomb and a Roman guard was put on duty.

Next, we have a problem with the way the missing body is discovered and reported to the disciples. And what can be said of the way Jesus appeared to the disciples, or of Thomas' initial doubt and subsequent belief? And would Jesus really have been walking round so confidently (and so fit) just days after the most brutal torture and near death? And if he had escaped death by means of trickery, the logical behaviour would have been to hide away. Yet he appeared to many disciples.

And finally, who were the fellow conspirators? They can only have been his disciples. Yet those same individuals went on to give the rest of their lives, and ultimately to die, for their faith in a resurrected Jesus. This is explored much more in the following chapters, but the conspiracy theory really does not work.

Jesus as a deluded individual?

Did Jesus think, wrongly, that he was God? This comes up against the same problems as the claim that Jesus was somehow a clever illusionist.

It is not beyond reason to argue that an individual might delude himself and might thereby exude an amazing feeling of power. At a stretch, that might explain healings of certain illnesses, at least some that have a psychological basis, that are perhaps emotional or "psychosomatic".

But read through the gospel accounts and it is immediately clear that this is a wholly inadequate explanation of most of the miracles described. The raising of the dead, the act of giving sight to the blind, the calming of the storm, the healing of the long-term sick and, in particular, the resurrection, are all totally incapable of being explained away in this manner. And so too are many of the other miracles.

Again, this hypothesis does not hold water.

Myth?

For the non-believer, this therefore leaves the idea that the stories are in the end no more than a myth, invented by those who first wrote them down. How convincingly is it possible to argue in this way?

Dating the four gospel accounts of Jesus' life is not easy[12] but it is generally accepted that Mark's narrative was completed within about 35 years of Jesus' death and that the latest of the four gospels was written within a further 25 years or so. Most, or probably all, of the four accounts were written just about within living memory of the events they describe concerning Jesus' ministry and death. Imagine writing a detailed account now of a well known individual who lived say 50 years ago and inventing stories that that individual had performed not just one or two but dozens of miraculous healings and other events; it simply would not work: the account would be laughed off as nonsense and would be rapidly forgotten.

It might be argued that the gospels contain true details of some of Jesus' life and teachings but that the miracle accounts were added for impact or for some political or other reason. There are plenty of people around who consider themselves Christian in at least some loose sense but who do not truly believe in miracles; but that does not work – you cannot be a Christian and not believe in miracles.

It makes no sense at all that the gospels should have accurately recorded certain aspects of the story of Jesus Christ but then embellished those stories with accounts of wholly fictional "miracles".

The miracles form such a huge part of the four gospels that the latter become meaningless without them. Fundamentally, if there was no resurrection then there is no Christianity at all, but the "lesser" miracles, too, are at the core of the accounts of Jesus' life. If he did not perform the miraculous healings, then why were the crowds following him so fervently? If he did not heal a man on the Sabbath, then why the argument with the authorities (see, for example, Matthew 12)? If he did not calm the storm then was the crossing of the lake a mere invention (Luke 8)? The miracles cannot be seen just as the icing on the cake of the gospels – they are at the heart of what the accounts of Jesus are telling us. If we throw out the miracles, we really have to throw out the gospels altogether; in Mark's account, for example, miracles form a key part of every one of the first ten chapters. It is surely a nonsense to reject the miracles whilst continuing to argue that the gospels give an otherwise accurate record of Jesus' life.

But there is a bigger argument than this. If Jesus existed, but was an ordinary man, then the actions of the early Christians are wholly inexplicable. This is explored in the next chapter.

+ + +

Chapter 3

~ The first Christians: external evidence ~

The first chapter contained a quotation by the Roman historian Tacitus who wrote about the fire that devastated Rome some 30 years after Jesus' death. Tacitus explained how the emperor Nero subsequently blamed the Christians: "Nero fastened the guilt . . . on a class hated for their abominations, called Christians by the populace."

Nero was an unpleasant character by all accounts, ruling with a ruthless and violent nature. It is reported that he murdered his first wife, kicked his second wife to death when she was pregnant and arranged the murder of his own mother. The idea that he fiddled while Rome burned is mythical but it is clear from historical records that he was brutal and unpredictable.

The view that the Christians were really responsible for the fire that devastated so much of Rome is not seriously held by anybody; in times of trouble one of the oldest tricks in the book is to blame an underdog. Of greater interest is the motivation of those who brought themselves to the attention of the authorities at a time when justice was very rough indeed. Even in a liberal western democracy in the twenty-first century it is no fun being part of a minority; human prejudices run deep and members of minority groups often suffer because of the failings or attitudes of a few. How much harder it must have been to subscribe to an idea that was deemed provocative both to the official political establishment and to the religion of those who were living under Roman occupation.

Yet the Tacitus document tells us that just one generation after Jesus' death, whilst many were still alive who would have seen Jesus on a day to day basis, and who were fully aware of his crucifixion, there were believers in different parts of the Roman empire and even in Rome itself. Something, therefore, persuaded these people that they should continue to believe in a man who had in human terms been dead for 30 years. Furthermore, they took this line even though (as we are told) they were hated for doing so, to the point of being used by a cowardly emperor as an easy scapegoat. And we are not talking here of a few individuals but of a "vast multitude" [13].

Without being unduly gruesome about it, it is worth pondering just how strong the faith of these people must have been. They faced not only the end of their lives here on earth but any of a wide range of methods of killing where each was more humiliating and barbaric than the last; death through the actions of dogs or lions or by crucifixion were just a few examples. See, for example, the final part of an article on miracles quoted on the website of the Catholic Education Resource Center [14].

Yet still the faith persisted and grew. The Pliny letter we have already quoted shows that the early development of Christianity continued apace. Pliny the Younger, a Roman governor in Asia Minor, was responsible for condemning to death those who were convicted of being Christians. As already noted in Chapter 1, he was checking up on how he was meant to deal with the developing faith because of the large numbers of men, women and children who called themselves Christians.

The passage quoted in Chapter 1 confirms some of the key points of the gospels and shows us that within perhaps 70 years of Jesus' death, large numbers of people were convinced enough of the Christian message to die for their faith. Under threat of torture or death, some not surprisingly renounced their faith but many others persisted. Pliny did not hesitate to condemn the latter to death, arguing that they deserved punishment for their sheer stubbornness.

So there is external evidence that confirms several of the key facts of the Christian message, including the existence of Christ as a real person, the early recognition of him as God, the practice of a high moral code, Jesus' death at the hands of Pontius Pilate and, by implication, the fact that something extraordinary happened to persuade people to follow his teaching at huge personal cost.

If Christ was not a truly extraordinary individual, if he did not die on the cross, and if he was not resurrected then what was it that kick-started the Christian religion? What happened, against all the odds and under the most brutal of regimes, that persuaded thousands upon thousands of people that it was all worth it? What persuaded them that they should commit no "evil actions", that they should speak the truth at all times and at whatever cost, and that they should ultimately accept torture and an appalling death rather than deny what they believed?

It is easy in our time to be cynical about these matters, for many states manipulate religious beliefs for political purposes, but that was not the case for these first century Christians – there was no state in the world where Christianity had even been recognised, never mind enforced. These were individuals who were prepared to swim against the most dangerous of tides because, with a simple and passionate faith, they believed strongly enough that Jesus Christ had died and had risen again from the dead.

+ + +

Chapter 4

~ The first Christians: Jesus' closest followers ~

So was the resurrection simply a myth created by a small group of Jesus' close disciples? There are several problems with this.

For a start, there is the whole question of motivation. Why invent the story when there was nothing to gain and all to lose? For Jesus' closest followers, or "disciples", had more to fear than anyone else, having been seen in public with Jesus over several years. Their best hope of survival would surely have been to lie low and to get back into their fishing or other livelihoods. They would have endured some mockery, no doubt, but life would have gone on. If they believed the evidence of their eyes that their Christian dream had come to an abrupt end on the cross then what did they possibly have to gain from claiming that Jesus was alive again?

And if they did invent the story, it was the biggest lie in history. They could not begin to foresee the consequences of what they were saying, it is true, but what a preposterous lie it would have been; how on earth did they convince the thousands who were prepared to give their lives for that story in the earliest decades after Jesus' death? That death on the cross was a most public event and, even against the background of familiar Roman brutality, must have been the talk of the town. As a man named Cleopas says, on the day of the resurrection but before he is aware of it, "You must be the only person staying in Jerusalem who does not know the things that have been happening there these last few days" [(15)].

And yet, as we have seen, thousands were prepared to die a horrible death rather then renounce their belief. If it was all untrue, then what was it that Jesus' closest followers said that convinced those people? A collection of mostly country people whose hero had just been seen to die in agony somehow managed to persuade thousands of others that that hero was worth dying for.

The idea that the followers invented a lie is in any case clearly nonsensical when we see what they themselves did with the rest of their lives. It is not difficult to imagine the feelings of the disciples in the days immediately following Jesus' death. They had spent three years with this amazing man, and had witnessed his inspired teaching and the many miracles that he had performed, including startling healings and the raising of two individuals from the dead. Yet they had now seen him mocked, tortured and killed. They were, very naturally, confused and scared.

Matthew tells us how Peter was challenged, soon after Jesus was arrested. Terrified, he denied having anything to do with him, not once but three times. The last of the gospels, written by John, tells us that shortly after Jesus' death, the disciples were hiding in a locked room, again out of fear of being discovered and of suffering a similar fate to that of Jesus himself.

So shortly after Jesus' death there is a group of terrified individuals, hiding themselves away from everyone else. Within months or years, these same individuals had the strength and courage to talk out about what they had seen, to devote the rest of their lives to promoting Jesus' message, and in most cases to give their lives for their faith. So what brought this transformation about?

First, according to the Bible, it was the re-appearance of Jesus himself. All four gospels recount how Jesus appeared after his death to his disciples. The first chapter of the *Acts of the Apostles*, too, tells us that Jesus presented himself "many times" to his disciples after his death. But is the argument simply circular for the non-believer who will by definition reject the idea that Jesus himself re-appeared? Fair enough, as long as there is a better explanation, but somehow we have to get from the starting point (an entirely plausible account of a group of frightened individuals) to the historically undeniable fact that Christianity became established and grew in the most hostile of environments.

But there was another force at work too. The second chapter of *Acts* describes how the apostles were all together at Pentecost, seven weeks after Easter, when the Holy Spirit came down onto them in the form of tongues of fire. We will look in more detail at the Holy Spirit in a later chapter – of the three "persons" of God, He can be the most difficult for the non-Christian to understand – but for the moment we stay with the earliest days of the Church. For now, we need to know only that – according to *Acts* – the Holy Spirit enabled the disciples to speak in a language that was understood by all the foreigners present and to work "many signs and miracles". Those who witnessed the events committed themselves to the Christian message in huge numbers, with around 3,000 baptisms in a single day.

But what was the fate of the twelve disciples themselves, chosen by Jesus to be his companions and to spread the news? These are listed[16] as Simon (known later as Peter), James and his brother John, Andrew, Philip, Bartholomew, Matthew, Thomas, another James, Thaddaeus, Simon the Zealot and Judas Iscariot. Judas betrayed Jesus but it is interesting to see whether the others stood by their beliefs in the aftermath of the crucifixion.

- Simon was a colourful character about whom much is said in the bible. He was named Peter by Jesus who told him that he was the rock on which he would build his church ("Peter" meaning "rock"). The Vatican basilica of St Peter is built upon the place where he was martyred. The fact that he lived and died as a Christian martyr in Rome is very extensively documented[17].

- St James died for the faith in 44 AD, under the orders of Herod Agrippa 1, grandson of Herod the Great. It is recorded in *Acts* 12 that he was beheaded.

- St John was the writer of the fourth of the gospels, and gave the rest of his life to the work of spreading the gospel message. He lived to a great age but the exact circumstances of his death are unknown; many believe that he had a miraculous escape and that he was the only one of the twelve who did not suffer a violent death.

- St Andrew is believed to have died by crucifixion during the reign of Nero, tradition having it that he was bound to the cross instead of being nailed to it – not an act of kindness but intended rather to prolong the painful death. The cross is thought to have been fixed transversely into the ground.

- The story of Philip, who may also have been known as Nathaniel, is less clear. Possibly he was crucified but other accounts suggest that he may have been beheaded. One way or another, there is good evidence that he died for his faith.

So too with the rest of the disciples, many crucified and others suffering different cruel fates[18]. The key point is that of the apostles chosen by Jesus all but the one who betrayed him devoted the rest of their lives to spreading the gospel message, often alone and in unfamiliar parts of the world. So we do not have here a politically motivated group who manipulated young and impressionable individuals to go out and die for their faith whilst they themselves watched from a safe distance. Rather, in every case except Judas, the apostles practised what they preached, giving everything including usually their very lives. If the message was untrue then the actions seem inexplicable.

+ + +

Chapter 5

~ Miracles today ~

We have looked at some of the miracles that Christians believe were performed by Jesus himself, or in connection with his appearance on earth. But those accounts of miracles were not the beginning. In the old testament, covering the centuries before the birth of Jesus, we read of how Moses led a passage for the Israelites across dry land through the middle of the Red Sea (Exodus 14), with a wall of water on either side of them. When the people were starving in the desert, God sent "manna" for them to eat (daily for 40 years!) – a literal feeding but also, for Christians, a forerunner of the new testament "bread from heaven" of Jesus Christ himself (Exodus 16). The book of Kings (Chapter 4) describes how large numbers of men are fed from a small amount of food, a miracle repeated on a greater scale in the new testament account of the feeding of the five thousand.

But if miracles really did happen in biblical times, why do they not happen now? We should probably begin by asking what we mean by "a miracle". In the bible, the issue is fairly clear cut but how would we understand the term today? Definitions abound, but I propose to think of a miracle as an event that has three features:

- it cannot reasonably be explained by rational means;
- it has a positive outcome;
- there is a clear association with prayer or with some other deliberate invocation of divine intervention.

So why do miracles, as thus defined, not take place today? Or do they? Is there even overwhelming evidence that events that meet these three criteria do occur, and actually quite frequently? Occurrences that cannot rationally be explained are the common thread running through the whole of this booklet. But for the moment let us focus on one-off events.

As the third leg of the above definition, it was suggested that there must be a clear association with prayer. Considerable care is needed here about the concept of prayer. It is easy to view God as some sort of glorified drinks machine – we pop our prayer token into the slot and expect the required item to come out at the bottom. But prayer simply does not work like that. The item does not appear and we conclude that the machine is broken, that prayer "doesn't work".

For the Christian, prayer is about building a relationship or, as it has been described, "the raising of the heart and mind to God". Suppose that a teenager behaves in a way that damages himself and other people that he meets, and that he then makes an insincere or even menacing request to his parents for money for a night out. The loving response from the parents may well be to deny him what he thinks he needs.

But that is an extreme example, of course. What about the devout and loving person praying selflessly, perhaps for a sick relative? Does prayer then have any effect?

The Christian believes that all prayer *is* heard and that all sincere prayer is answered, though often not in the way we anticipate or indeed wish. Even fervent prayers from good people do not always *seem* to be answered. We revert later in this booklet to the question of suffering, where perhaps the greatest challenges arise for the Christian. For the moment, suffice it to say that as Christians we believe that there is a much bigger picture than we can see, and that there is a spiritual dimension – beyond our limited perception – that will ultimately put all our human activities into a very different perspective. These questions lead us into much deeper (and ultimately more interesting) issues but away from the direction of the present argument.

Let us simply accept, for now, that miraculous events do not routinely occur on demand, at least in the way that is being expected. But that proves very little one way or the other. The more relevant question for present purposes is whether *any* miracles take place; if they do then the onus is on the non-believer to provide a rational explanation. That is a very different proposition and there is a danger of a false circle of denial here: "God does not exist, so miracles cannot happen, so anything that says that miracles happen is self-evidently false, so it is not even worth considering the evidence."

A good example of a living person whose life has witnessed (and participated in) many miracles is an Irish nun by the name of Sister Briege McKenna. (The internet provides plenty of background material for anyone wishing to look further into her life and claims.) I have not personally met her, but I know several people who have and they invariably hold her in great esteem.

Sister McKenna herself had severe rheumatoid arthritis as a teenager and in her early 20s and wore casts for nearly three years. She was at a spiritual retreat in 1970 and was praying not for a physical cure for her condition but for the chance to grow and deepen her faith with which she was struggling. She ended up getting more than she had bargained for – the start of a lifetime healing ministry but also an instant and total cure of her own condition. Sister McKenna describes this event, and many that followed, in her book *Miracles Do Happen*[19].

If we begin with the story of her own healing, we again have a choice to make. As presented in her book, the nun had a debilitating illness over a period of several years, requiring serious medical intervention. Overnight, as it were, the illness disappeared and never returned. What are the options for the cynic? A straight lie? This is not a rational explanation – here is an individual who was living in a community, who had received medical tests and so on; there can really be no doubt that this woman was seriously ill at some point. Equally, it is obvious that she has lived for many years since without any trace of the illness, so there was definitely a cure, and a fast one at that.

Perhaps Sister Briege simply underwent a medical operation of some sort? This does not work: even if such a cure existed for such an illness, Sister Briege is a well known figure who has spoken openly of her healing; if there were anything fraudulent in that claim then a doctor or nurse or someone else in the know would have made that fact public years ago.

So what other "rational" explanations exist? Perhaps it was a psychosomatic illness? This seems totally implausible for a case of severe rheumatoid arthritis, lasting for several years and subject to medical intervention. A claim that an illness was somehow just the result of a mental condition is often the last roll of the dice for those seeking a rational explanation where all else fails. But why did the cure come at just that moment? And even if it seemed a plausible explanation, it is then necessary to explain how the same individual comes to be associated with so many cures of other people over the decades that follow.

The book *Miracles Do Happen* is much more than just a list of inexplicable happenings – the main part of the text is an intelligent analysis of Sister Briege's own spiritual development in the context of her mission of healing. The miracles themselves are used to illustrate particular points that she is making and one suspects that those recorded in the book (which was in any case published some 20 years ago) are only the tip of the iceberg of the healings she has witnessed; indeed, some of the websites that talk about her work confirm this. Other examples she gives, though, include a young child with severe burns who is placed under the altar during a celebration of Mass in a remote part of South America and who is running around unhurt an hour later.

Then there is a woman with such advanced stomach cancer that the doctors said they would be unable to operate, who came to Sister Briege to ask for help in her terror of facing death. On Sister Briege's advice, and supported by her prayer, the woman went to Holy Communion that same day and sensed an overwhelming experience at the moment of taking the Host into her mouth ("I had no sooner put the Host on my tongue and swallowed it than I felt as though something was burning my throat and down into my stomach. I looked down at my stomach and the growth was gone.") She was found immediately afterwards to be totally cured.

And so on. Lots of cures. Men, women, children. The only common threads are faith and prayer.

And Sister Briege is just one example among many. The book *The Happiest People on Earth*[20] is full of extraordinary accounts of Christians at the other end of the spectrum, as it were, from the Catholic church of which Sister Briege is a member. The book concerns a group of Armenian families who emigrate to America. One particular family builds up a thriving dairy farming business, operating all the while in the context of a deep Christian faith. One member of the family, Demos Shakarian sets up a group that addresses business people throughout the world on Christian issues. The story of how the family business grows from nothing, whilst always consciously putting God at the heart of everything, is extraordinary in itself. Along the way, there are numerous stories of inexplicable happenings, including healings of humans and, at least once, of animals, as well as many other events that defy rational explanation.

These are just two extreme examples of individuals who have been associated with enough miraculous events to merit whole books about them. There are, in fact, many healing ministries taking place in the UK in the twenty-first century. If we then add to this list the happenings at Lourdes and elsewhere (see Chapter 6), the person of Padre Pio (see Chapter 8), the incidents described in Chapter 7 re the workings of the Holy Spirit, and so on, then the weight of evidence for supernatural, prayer-linked happenings seems overwhelming.

+ + +

Chapter 6

~ Visions and apparitions ~

Introduction

Much of what is heard or reported about apparitions and ghostly experiences is clearly nonsense. There is something depressing about a piece of toast reportedly sold on Ebay for a huge sum because the toasting process appears to have imprinted Jesus' face on it. Similarly, the whole question of "coincidence" can be nothing more than a failure to understand statistical probability or a failure to gain a perspective on something in which one happens to be personally involved.

But in the realm of Christian visions and apparitions, is there a danger of throwing the baby out with the bathwater, of failing to spot the gold nuggets amongst the dross?

Nobody is *required* to believe in apparitions of the Virgin Mary. To some readers, that is perhaps an odd statement, but those who wish to belong to the Catholic church, for example, are expected to hold to certain fundamental beliefs: the divinity of Christ, the concept of the Holy Trinity, the resurrection of Christ, to give but a few examples. There is no equivalent requirement that anybody should accept the truth of the visions and apparitions that are reported to have taken place at various times and in various locations, even in the cases that have been exhaustively and rigorously scrutinised by the church authorities.

For me personally, these visions and apparitions form a rather small part of what and why I believe; I find that I do not really need them as part of the base on which to build my belief. Nevertheless, there are some remarkable accounts that yet again pose difficulties for those who would argue from a strict rationalist perspective.

It is worth mentioning here that some non-Catholics argue that Christian faith must be built on the words of the bible alone, and that any form of ongoing revelation is by definition untrue. They would therefore reject out of hand the idea that God might somehow continue to communicate with his people, whether through apparitions or otherwise. (As a "convert" to Catholicism some 20 years ago, I would not share that view; the reasons are long and complex and out of place here but the feeling is rather that of having moved from two to three dimensions in my faith, or from black and white to colour.) But anyone may of course choose to reject the accounts given in this chapter, provided only that they can find a reasoned basis to do so.

Lourdes

The story of Lourdes is familiar to many. In 1858, a poor fourteen year old girl, Bernadette Soubirous, claimed to have visions of the Virgin Mary ("a beautiful lady"). Mocked by all around her, she stuck to her story. One day, the lady told her to drink water from the spring but there was no spring to be seen. On a sign from the lady, Bernadette clawed at the earth with her bare hands until a spring burst forth.

For our purposes, the real question is how much credence a sceptic in the twenty-first century can give to such events. Perhaps Bernadette was, after all, simply the "very impressionable" girl that Dawkins claims her (in his television programmes of early January 2006) to have been.

The fame of Lourdes revolves around its cures. Shortly after the initial visions, a young boy's failing eyesight is said to have been cured after applying the water from the spring. Since then, many millions of people have visited the shrine that was established at the site of the visions and there are detailed records of many thousands of physical cures. Commercialism has inevitably taken over to some extent the whole experience of visiting Lourdes. But the fact that commercial interests have hurried to exploit the phenomenon tells us nothing either for or against its underlying truth.

Many who attend the site claim to have experienced *spiritual* (rather than physical) healing but the atheist will of course dismiss such healing as nonsense, so the whole debate becomes circular: if you believe in God you can believe in spiritual healing but if you are an atheist you do not. The atheist will assume that such healing claims are either imagined or are no more than a 'placebo effect'. For believers, spiritual healing is of the utmost importance. But as a building block in an argument for the existence of God it can have no place.

But what of physical healing? The Catholic encyclopaedia[21] contains an account by one Georges Bertrin who devoted the greater part of his life to observing the events at Lourdes during the first 50 years in which it was an established point of pilgrimage. Bertrin explains how for those first five decades of the shrine's existence he recorded every recovery and reached a figure of 3,962, a figure considered in reality (for reasons explained in the article) to be considerably less than the actual number of cures. Bertrin records that the cures included healings from tuberculosis, tumours, sores, cancers, deafness, blindness, and a range of other maladies.

Bertrin then quotes the *Annales des Sciences Physiques*, a sceptical review by one Dr Richet, Professor at the Medical Faculty of Paris, who wrote of the study that "on reading it, unprejudiced minds cannot but be convinced that the facts stated are authentic".

It may well be argued that 4,000 physical cures (or indeed, say, 40,000, if the true figure is dramatically higher) is a small number out of several million visitors in the first 50 years of pilgrimage to this site. It is doubtless true that many have visited the site in vain for a physical cure.

The believer will say that all visitors who go there in the right frame of mind perhaps come away with a cure of some sort, be it physical, mental or spiritual. This argument will obviously be rejected by the atheist but Lourdes nevertheless poses a problem for the non-believer as millions will attest to their belief that something extraordinary is taking place there and there are (at least) thousands of unexplained cures for which such ideas as the placebo effect, or auto-suggestion, or indeed fluke, offer no adequate explanation. But Lourdes is really just the beginning; indeed, as an argument to put in the balance when seeking the truth about these matters it probably carries little weight, if only because the events took place so long ago.

Fatima

The Lourdes phenomenon is far from unique. Marian apparitions, as these sightings of the Virgin Mary are known, have been reported in many corners of the world. Another famous series of visions was in Portugal, at Fatima. Here, three young shepherd children (none over the age of 10) saw visions of Mary over a period of six months in 1917, also receiving three "secrets".

The children were subjected to some ferocious questioning by the local authorities; the provincial administrator, determined to find out the nature of the secrets, imprisoned them and separated the children, telling each that the others had been boiled to death in oil. He failed to persuade the youngsters to divulge the secrets.

These visions took place on the same day each month (apart from a variation when the children were imprisoned) and before the last the children had announced that a miracle would occur on that day, 13 October. As a result, and despite a thunderstorm with torrential rain, there were some 70,000 people present, including reporters from many of the country's leading newspapers.

After the heavy rain, the sun was seen to make extraordinary movements in the sky. The online *Wikipedia* encyclopaedia[22] tells how some of the country's newspapers reported the events:

Portugal's most influential newspaper was said to be *O Século*, reputedly strongly anti-clerical. Its columnist reported that:

> "Before the astonished eyes of the crowd, whose aspect was biblical as they stood bare-headed, eagerly searching the sky, the sun trembled, made sudden incredible movements outside all cosmic laws – the sun 'danced' according to the typical expression of the people."

The Lisbon paper *O Dia* reported:

> "The silver sun, enveloped in the same gauzy grey light, was seen to whirl and turn in the circle of broken clouds... . The light turned a beautiful blue, as if it had come through the stained-glass windows of a cathedral, and spread itself over the people who knelt with outstretched hands ... people wept and prayed with uncovered heads, in the presence of a miracle they had awaited."

And *Wikipedia* also reports the account of a doctor, an eye specialist, writing for a newspaper *Ordem*:

> "The sun, at one moment surrounded with scarlet flame, at another aureoled in yellow and deep purple, seemed to be in an exceeding fast and whirling movement, at times appearing to be loosened from the sky and to be approaching the earth, strongly radiating heat."

At the end of it all, the clothes of the people – so recently sodden – were completely dry. Scientists detected no unusual weather phenomenon on that day. Further accounts can be found online[23]. The events were reported in newspapers worldwide.

Two of the children died whilst still very young. The last, Lucia Santos – aged 10 at the time of the visions – became a nun and survived to an old age, dying in February 2005.

What "rational" explanation can be given for these events? It has been suggested that there was simply a "coronal mass ejection" from the sun (as in fact occurred, for example, on 13 May 2000). These events are violent ejections of material from the outer atmosphere of the sun, often causing major geomagnetic storms. Yet:

- here an event occurred, the timing of which was precisely predicted by three peasant children (and matched the day on which they had reported visions in the preceding months);
- it is specifically reported that there were no recorded meteorological phenomena on the day in question; and
- the "mass ejection" theory cannot explain how people's clothes were immediately dry.

The surviving child decided to devote the rest of her life to her faith (and, incidentally, had meetings with many popes, including a special spiritual relationship with the late John Paul II). It seems clear that she, at least, believed wholeheartedly in what she had witnessed.

Medjugorje

The next apparitions to be considered here have continued right up to the present, in Medjugorje in Bosnia Herzegovina. Some people believe the whole thing to be an elaborate and prolonged hoax. There are without doubt issues of church politics here but the politics may be at least as much on the side of the doubters as on that of those who believe in these events.

The Medjugorje visions began on 24 June 1981. Six children claimed to have seen the Virgin Mary, proclaiming a message of peace. Messages are given on a daily basis and the children were also each given ten "secrets" about future events, in some cases of worldwide significance but in other cases of a much more personal nature. The essential message, though, is a call for people to commit back to their faith and a call for the faithful to pray, to fast, to read the bible, to go to the sacrament of reconciliation (confession) and to receive Holy Communion.

In the 26 years since the visions began, more than 30 million pilgrims and other curious visitors have been to the village. Healings of body, spirit and mind have been reported in great numbers. For believers, these – and the messages from Mary – are of the greatest interest.

The sceptic will have other priorities. Full details of the claims that are made about the Medjugorje apparitions can be found at the official website, and especially at the page of "frequently asked questions"[24]. Some of the supernatural phenomena reported by the people at large mirror the events of Fatima of October 1917: the sun being seen to "dance", the ability of the people to look at the sun without hurting their eyes, and so on.

Those who believe that the whole Medjugorje phenomenon is a hoax are saying that a story was invented by six children (aged between 10 and 16 when the visions began) in June 1981, and that all six of the children have stuck to the story throughout the intervening period, even though most have since married and have children of their own, and all have been subjected to many rigorous examinations over the years. It really beggars belief to imagine that all six children would maintain a fantasy into adulthood, or that six would all be taken in by the same imagined vision at the same time.

These details barely scratch the surface of the events reported at Medjugorje. Anyone interested should go to the website, which is well laid out and which contains reams of further details about the whole phenomenon. Yet again, any fair observer would admit – at the very least – that there is something remarkable here.

St Faustina

Sister Faustina was canonised (i.e. to become Saint Faustina) in April 2000. She was a twentieth century Polish nun who had died in Krakow at the age of 33. I propose to say little about her, except that she had visions of Jesus Christ, who revealed to her a message (and prayer) of Divine Mercy. In essence, we are invited once more to turn to God and to trust in His mercy and compassion[25].

In a sense, Faustina's story falls outside the context of this booklet; her life as a nun, suffering from severe ill health for much of her short adult life, perhaps had little that would offer a "wow" factor to persuade the non-believer. But Sister Faustina's prayer, known as the Chaplet of Divine Mercy, is simple and quite short (it lasts about five minutes) and is suitable for any child or adult who would like to try a short meditative prayer. The chaplet can be found online[26].

For those who do believe, the promises associated with the prayer are powerful. Faustina records Jesus' words to her on the subject as follows:

> "Say unceasingly this chaplet that I have taught you.
>
> Anyone who says it will receive great Mercy at the hour of death.
>
> Priests will recommend it to sinners as the last hope.
>
> Even the most hardened sinner, if he recites this Chaplet even once, will receive grace from My Infinite Mercy.
>
> I want the whole world to know My Infinite Mercy.
>
> I want to give unimaginable graces to those who trust in My Mercy."

For a person who honestly cannot believe in the Christian message at all, and for whom the message of this booklet carries no weight, these words may seem empty. But they offer a wonderful turning point for anyone who fundamentally believes, or who at least wishes to re-consider the whole question of their belief, but whose faith has been neglected or buried under the troubles, or pleasures, of everyday life.

Associated with this prayer is a picture that depicts Jesus as seen in St Faustina's visions. The picture has, in its English translation, the words "Jesus, I Trust in You". It can now be found in many Catholic churches across the world.

Other accounts

A few examples have been given above of sites where visions and apparitions have been said to take place. The ones referred to are well known and have been subject to particularly intensive scrutiny over the years. Nevertheless, they are only a few of many. Another recent example has been in Sievernich, near Cologne, in Germany.

It has to be recognised that this is fertile territory for falsehoods and delusions. As such, it is at least as harmful for the believer to embrace every account with unguarded enthusiasm as it is for the sceptic to reject everything out of hand – reason has to be brought into play on both sides. But the fact that some accounts may be false does not mean that they all are. The Catholic church is far from jumping on the bandwagon of every reported sighting, subjecting all serious reports to rigorous and lengthy scrutiny and encouraging discernment and caution on the part of its members.

Chapter 7

~ The Holy Spirit – the gift of tongues ~

The Holy Spirit is, in Christian belief, one of the three persons of God: in a way we do not claim to understand fully, we profess a belief in God the Father, God the Son (Jesus) and God the Holy Spirit (or, in some translations, God the Holy Ghost). Together, these make up the Holy Trinity.

The Holy Spirit can perhaps be the most difficult of the three with which to identify. As children, Christians (along with the holders of many other monotheistic beliefs) perhaps gain some view of an elderly, bearded man which represents (albeit in a hopelessly inadequate way) God the Father: we can gain some image to hold in our minds. Picturing God the Son is easy: at once God and man, we can at least imagine the man and we are helped in this by films and by artistic representations of the person of Jesus. But God the Holy Spirit? That is a much more difficult proposition: what image can we hold that can begin to help us to understand this most ethereal part of the Holy Trinity?

Despite the difficulty of picturing a spirit, it is worth persevering. For the atheist, or the serious doubter, the Holy Spirit is a great place to start. Phenomenal events are taking place in the name of the Holy Spirit, throughout the world and in all the Christian churches. Furthermore, these events are occurring with ever greater frequency: this truly seems to be an aspect of the Christian church that is more real and more alive today than it was a generation or two ago.

But first some background. The Holy Spirit is at the heart of Christian belief and solidly founded in biblical teaching. Baptism is given in the name of the Father, the Son and the Holy Spirit (Matthew 28:19); Mary the Virgin conceived Jesus through the power of the Holy Spirit (Luke 1:35); the Holy Spirit is fundamentally involved in sanctifying us (1 Corinthians

3:16, 6:11) and in bringing God's love to us (Romans 5:5); the Holy Spirit is linked closely to spiritual wisdom and to faith (Acts 6:3-5) and specifically to the instruction of the faith (John 14:26). We are also told that there are gifts of the Holy Spirit that are given separately to individuals: to one person the gift might be wisdom, to another knowledge, or faith, or the grace of healing, or the power to work miracles, or the gift of prophecy, or the discerning of spirits, or the gift of tongues or the interpretation of speeches (1 Corinthians 12:3-11; Acts 2:4).

But what does all this mean for an agnostic, in modern times? To answer this, consider the gifts just listed. For the believer, wisdom or knowledge or (especially) faith would be the most valuable gifts. For the person who is searching for an answer as to whether it is all true, the gifts of healing, the working of miracles and the act of speaking in tongues will be more important as they can be more objectively assessed and considered. The first two of these go together to some extent, if only in the sense that those who do not believe will often quote a genuine healing as the miracle that would make them change their minds. These are considered in much greater depth in many of the chapters of this booklet.

But what about this mysterious concept of "speaking in tongues"? In reality, this term may be used to mean several rather different things. First, there is the question of an individual speaking a real language that he has never learnt or at least of speaking in such a way as to be understood by people with whom the speaker has no common language. The bible records a dramatic incident of this[27].

But the term "speaking in tongues" (or "praying in the Spirit") can also be used in cases where individuals – invariably after actively inviting the Holy Spirit to be present in their lives – start to pray in a spiritual language that they themselves do not understand: effectively a form of prayer that transcends human language. As always, the internet can provide countless examples but this is something I have seen at first hand.

My first personal contact with this phenomenon was many years ago, when a university friend of mine – quietly spoken, rational, intelligent – recounted an incident she had just seen of someone speaking in tongues.

More recently, I have witnessed it even more closely on numerous occasions. First, this was through a parish priest whom we know well as a good family friend. He has his feet firmly on the ground as demonstrated in the way he runs the parish but also has the gift of speaking in tongues. What I mean by this is that, on particular occasions, he will speak – quietly but fluently – in a prayer language that he himself has never learnt and that he does not understand. He does this only in an appropriate context. If a parishioner asks for a blessing, for example, he will lay his hands on the individual and pray; first, it may be in English but then he will switch quietly but confidently into this unfamiliar language, before reverting to English to conclude the blessing. Always, he will be invoking the Holy Spirit as part of the prayer.

This is a very personal thing, in a way. I know this priest well and no "rational" explanation of the phenomenon of speaking an unknown language seems remotely satisfactory to me. For it to be fraudulent is out of the question in the context of what this man does with his life. For him to be deceiving himself is equally improbable – I have lived abroad at various times and, as a result, I speak three other European languages fairly fluently, but I cannot begin to string sentences together in a make-believe language in a way that sounds remotely convincing. This priest has many great qualities but speaking foreign languages is not among them.

My direct witnessing of this speaking in tongues is not, in any case, limited to this one individual. I have attended charismatic prayer groups at which I have witnessed the same in dozens of other individuals, and even a group singing spontaneously together in tongues.

It is fair to say that the idea of speaking in tongues is a source of some considerable disagreement in the Christian world – not so much between the various denominations, for the phenomenon can be seen in most or all of the Christian churches – but within the different branches themselves. The reason for this is perhaps that this is the most blatantly "irrational" happening that visibly and indisputably takes place in our churches and it therefore forces us in a special way to face up to something that we cannot explain. (Speaking in tongues is in fact much less miraculous than what Catholics understand to take place during the celebration of the Eucharist (Holy Communion) but it is more provocative in that it is there for all to see and hear.)

St Paul (who, incidentally, was a leading persecutor of the first Christians until his own extraordinary conversion) gives it an official seal of approval "I should like you all to speak in tongues"[28]. But its importance is nevertheless played down, as in his immediately following comment ("I would much rather that you could prophesy"). Arguably, St Paul would take a different view now as his preference for prophesy was that it seemed to be the better tool for building up the church; in our time, the gift of speaking in tongues is playing an important role in doing just that. Nevertheless, Christianity tends to play down its significance – it is not for everybody and it has been described as the least important of the many gifts of the Holy Spirit. Yet the topic has its place in this booklet as a Christian phenomenon that can be witnessed.

So is there a rational explanation for this? I suppose the cynic's most likely answer would be some sort of mass hysteria, but for me that explanation just does not add up. Some of the incidents referred to above have indeed occurred in large groups and have been accompanied by music, both of which can perhaps be argued to encourage irrational behaviour in some cases. But I have also witnessed this at first hand in the most unemotional and normal circumstances, even within seconds of talking about completely mundane issues, and often where the individual is alone or in a small group.

The other possible explanation is some form of deception, whether of self or fraudulently of others; the reader who does not know the individuals concerned cannot, I suppose, rule that out altogether but for me it is an absolute non-starter. And I am not alone: the phrase "speaking in tongues" produces well over a million Google hits. Searches under such related topics as "Catholic charismatic renewal" also yield some interesting results.

Chapter 8

~ Stigmata ~

Introduction

A number of people over the centuries have borne the marks of Christ's suffering on their own bodies, known as stigmata. More specifically, well over 300 people are recorded as having had wounds on their bodies in the places where Jesus' body was pierced at the time of his crucifixion: hands, feet, side.

There can be no doubt about the existence of these marks in certain people – there is plenty of physical and photographic evidence from the 20th century and there are without doubt stigmatists alive today. The challenge for the non-believer is to find a satisfactory rational explanation.

Oldest examples

Although St Paul had written: "I bear in my body the marks of the Lord Jesus"[29], this is generally interpreted rather less literally than to say that he had the stigmata, though some have suggested that this is in fact the correct meaning. St Francis of Assisi, on the other hand, clearly bore the marks early in the thirteenth century and he is generally considered to be the first well documented case. The matter is well described on various websites, including the following:

> "[Francis] was in the middle of a 40-day fast, feeling weak, and his eyes were burning. While praying and concentrating on his meditations, Francis experienced a vision of an angel carrying an image of a man nailed to a cross. When the vision disappeared, Francis felt sharp pains in various places on his body. Looking to find the source, he realized that he had five marks like those on Jesus' hands, feet, and side" [30].

It is easy, however, for a sceptic to dismiss evidence from the thirteenth century, let alone an ambiguous reference from the first century. For a more recent example, the case of Padre Pio brings us well into the second half of the 20th century.

Padre Pio

A search on Google or any other search engine will provide massive amounts of information about this extraordinary man. So who was he and what place does he have in this narrative? Francesco Forgione was born in Pietrelcina, Italy, in 1887. He took the name Pio when he joined the Order of Friars Minor Capuchin at the age of 15, based at the monastery of San Giovanni Rotondo. He was ordained priest at age 23.

In the early years of his priesthood, and even before then, he had various mystical experiences. These included, early on, the stigmata, accompanied by severe pain. Pio found the visible signs of the stigmata to be both embarrassing and humiliating. He therefore prayed that the visible evidence should disappear, which it did until September 1918. The pain, however, continued – not only in his hands, feet and sides but also the pain of the crown of thorns and the scourging.

On 20 September 1918, when kneeling alone in the chapel, Pio had a vision of a mysterious person whose hands, feet and sides were dripping with blood. When the vision disappeared, Pio became aware that his own hands, feet and side had been pierced and were bleeding. This time, the visible bleeding wounds remained and they stayed with him for the rest of his life – fifty years and three days from that date.

So how to explain them? An American atheist website states that "there were claims that he ... had even inflicted stigmata wounds on himself using acid" [31]. The reference is made in an article dated as 2 May 1999 carrying a fairly vitriolic attack on the late John Paul II's beatification of Pio. The idea that the wounds were self-inflicted is an obvious line to explore. But there are many problems with it.

The Catholic church itself – perhaps contrary to what would be imagined – is the harshest critic of those within its ranks who claim to have witnessed, or to have been involved with, extraordinary supernatural phenomena. The Holy See launched two major investigations, and for a while confined Pio to near isolation within his religious community, refusing to accept that anything positive was taking place. But further evidence continued to emerge until, by 1934, the church had officially withdrawn all objections to his activities. Pope Pius XI commented that he had not been ill disposed towards Pio but merely ill informed. Further investigations were carried out at the time of Pio's beatification (as is always the case) and, of course, the fact that he was duly beatified and then canonised (to become St Pio) was the strongest indication that the church had accepted the events surrounding Pio as genuine.

There is then a real issue about motivation. Why would a man who devoted his whole life to the vows of poverty, chastity and obedience invent a lie and sustain it for five decades, not even renouncing it on his death bed when he was over 80 years old? This was a person who frequently spent 19 hours a day on his spiritual work (saying Mass, hearing confessions, replying to letters received from all over the world). It is recorded that he often slept for no more than two hours per night, that at times he subsisted for up to three weeks with no nourishment other than the Eucharist, and that he heard up to 25,000 confessions per year. It is difficult to reconcile the maintaining of a lie with an individual who was prepared to devote every waking hour to his spiritual duties for decades on end.

Next comes the matter of opportunity. How does an individual, living in a community of poverty and great simplicity, have the opportunity to inflict these wounds on himself? Where does the acid come from, with which he is supposed to have inflicted his own wounds? How does a man who was being rigorously investigated by religious and non-religious alike conceal that acid? Or were the wounds inflicted by some sort of weapon that was never found? Yet the wounds, which never ceased to bleed throughout the 50 years, never became infected. At the time of his death, they disappeared immediately and without any trace of scarring.

And then there is the fact that so many other spiritual gifts seem to have been given to Pio. There are healings, such as a Sicilian girl named Gemma di Giorgi who had been born without pupils but who gained her sight during a visit to Padre Pio. Another remarkable claim, but one regarding which there are numerous reports from many parts of the world, is that of "bi-location". Is it really possible that an individual can get so close to God that he can in this life overcome the constraints of time and space and be in two places at once? Perhaps that is too fantastical a claim for some, but readers who are interested can again find much further information online.

As always, the wealth of the Padre Pio experience for those who already believe does not lie in ever more amazing pointers to the existence of a loving Christian God. Rather, the value of his life and suffering is found in the renewal of faith that he engendered: the conversions, the vocations, the strengthening of personal faith. And, incidentally, he founded an important hospital; this man who understood how valuable suffering could become was nevertheless passionate about his Hospital for the Relief of Suffering, insisting that everyone who worked in it should have a full understanding of human dignity. *Wikipedia* describes it today as "one of the most efficient hospitals in Italy and Europe" [32].

Numbers are not a good proof of anything but there is no doubt that Padre Pio was well loved in his lifetime and continues to be the subject of much affection to this day. Around 100,000 mourners attended Padre Pio's funeral and visitors to San Giovanni Rotondo are said to outnumber even those who go to Lourdes. A member of the American 15th Air Force who first set eyes on Pio around the end of 1943 witnessed the agonising pain that the priest experienced during that central part of the Mass known as the consecration. The American commented simply that "I am a witness to a saint in formation. I was totally convinced that here was a priest who had attained a state of sanctity the like of which I had only read about, but never met before" [33].

But as far as the stigmata are concerned, Pio was just one of many.

Other stigmatists

The experiences of priests like Padre Pio have been shared by many others, of whom a large majority have been women [34]. See also *Stigmata and Modern Science* [35].

Another particularly remarkable example of a twentieth century stigmatist is Marthe Robin, a French woman who was born in 1902, was completely paralysed from the age of 26, was blind before the age of 40 and who for more than 50 years exhibited the signs of the stigmata on a weekly basis. She suffered intense pains each time, which she willingly accepted and offered up to Christ as a sharing in his own suffering.

With the sole exception of a weekly communion wafer, Marthe neither ate nor drank anything at all (and had no drip or other medical form of feeding) for more than five decades. This is clearly a remarkable miracle in itself.

A simple and short account of this woman's life can be found on the EWTN website [36]. In fact, accounts are to be found in huge numbers. See also, for example, the site of an organisation called *Christendom Awake* [37].

Moving into the twenty-first century, reports continue, including that of one Fra Elia, a stigmatist friar in Umbria in Italy. Details of this man are only just starting to emerge but there is some evidence that remarkable things are occurring in connection with him too.

+ + +

Chapter 9

~ Darwin and modern science ~

One of the big debates between believers and others is the question of creationism versus evolution. But I suggest that the issue is, for the Christian, not such an important one.

Those who argue in favour of the idea of a Creator often talk about evolution as if there is something "random" about it: how could an elephant or a fish or a human being come about just by chance? This, though, is a misrepresentation of what Darwinian evolution is all about. In very simplistic terms, Darwinian evolution can be reduced to two elements: natural selection and random mutations, but the combination of those two elements is far from random.

Natural selection is an appealing concept and is simply illustrated. Imagine a large herd of giraffes living a reasonably idyllic existence in an area with few predators. Disaster strikes in the form of a population explosion of another type of animal that eats the same food as the giraffes. Hunger takes hold and many giraffes die as a result. The taller giraffes, however, find that they can reach the leaves that the new animals cannot reach. As a result, more of the taller giraffes survive to adulthood and duly reproduce. On average, the offspring of the taller giraffes naturally tend in their turn to be taller than the offspring of any shorter giraffes. The cycle is repeated over several generations and even in a rather short space of time, the average height of the colony of giraffes may increase. The normal variations in height have led to a process of natural selection whereby the taller ones reproduce so that the average nature of the whole herd is changed. Nothing random or haphazard there.

The giraffe development – a purely theoretical one created for this purpose – is entirely plausible. Given the right circumstances, one might almost say that the outcome is predictable and self-evidently true. And there is nothing random about it at all.

The next stage of the Darwinian theory effectively states that that same process is carried out over millions and indeed billions of years. Darwin's theory was, after all, labelled *The Origin of Species* so it is concerned with much more than minor modifications. In the end, the argument is that everything that lives or has lived – a tree, a person, a dinosaur, a dog, a fly – is a development that has come about through this same process of random mutations and natural selection. Thus the theory is of huge numbers of tiny changes. As Darwin puts it:

> "For as all the inhabitants of each country are struggling together with nicely balanced forces, extremely slight modifications in the structure or habits of one inhabitant would often give it an advantage over others." [38]

> "As many more individuals of each species are born than can possibly survive; and as, consequently, there is a frequently recurring struggle for existence, it follows that any being, if it vary however slightly in any manner profitable to itself, under the complex and sometimes varying conditions of life, will have a better chance of surviving, and thus be naturally selected. From the strong principle of inheritance, any selected variety will tend to propagate its new and modified form." [39]

The question of the ultimate origin of all these life forms (did everything evolve from a single life-giving moment?) is touched on below. But first, it needs to be acknowledged that Darwinism is no more than a *theory* of how life has evolved. Few scientists would argue that it is a proven concept, though most would say that it is the best show in town, in the sense that the Darwinian theory stacks up better than any others. But the theory is not without its challenges.

One of the big problems of Darwinian theory is the complexity of developments. An often quoted example is the development of the eye. Dawkins takes the trouble to analyse the workings of the eye in some detail and I bow totally to his hugely superior scientific knowledge. To reduce his analysis to its simplest form, he refers to an electronic interface in the eye which contains around three million "ganglion cells" and advises us that these cells gather data from about 125 million photocells. A more detailed description is then given of these photocells, still astoundingly complex and containing mitochondria which process more than 700 different chemical substances[40].

It is worth pausing here to note in passing that evolutionists accept that the eye has developed independently in different species, so somehow this level of complexity is said to have evolved more than once.

An argument *against* evolution, of course, is that without this massively complex combination of cells, the eye is useless. Darwinian theory must hypothesise that on "day x" there is an organism that has no photocell but somehow on "day x plus one" either that organism or its immediate offspring has a photocell: fair enough. That photocell, though, must then give the organism an advantage over all of the otherwise similar organisms so that, somehow, the organism with the photocell is more likely to survive long enough to replicate itself and create another organism with a photocell. Furthermore, that advantage must be sufficient so that over time the organisms without a photocell die out or, at least, develop along a different path so as to become a separate species.

The organism with the photocell, meanwhile, must somehow mutate once more so that it has not one such cell but two, then three and then an explosion of such cells. And along the way, it must leap through enough genetic mutations to develop the astounding complexity that is the modern eye.

The development described in very simplistic terms above must involve the gaining of a genetic advantage at every stage of development: without that, the slightly modified organism will never surge ahead in the genetic race. But how can the development of the single photocell serve any useful function on its own, i.e. (for example) without some sort of brain or simple processor? Dawkins states that "some single-celled animals have a light-sensitive spot" and argues, broadly, that any light sensitivity is better than none. But this solution seems very problematic. Scientists have different views about how far back the eye started to develop but let us assume that it was a very long way back indeed, in some unsophisticated creature which (as Darwin would have it) eventually developed into human beings. Suppose, then, that a genetic mutation caused the development of a single light-sensitive cell. If we have 125 million photocells, it is difficult for us to imagine how small the difference must be between having no sight and having a single photo-sensitive cell. Yet the hypothesis must be that this tiny step must have given some real genetic advantage to a simple organism even though, by definition, the brain of the organism would have no machinery for interpreting the light or knowing its significance.

A further problem for the evolution theory is that of sexuality. Using the same concept as before, we must hypothesise that on "day x" there was no sex anywhere in the world but that on "day x plus one" there was. The difficulty is that two asexual creatures must have developed – not over millions of years but at the same moment and in the same place – so that one was able to act as male and the other as female. And they must have known what they had to do and how to do it!

Dawkins and others have considered these issues and have obviously satisfied themselves that the problems are not insoluble from a scientific point of view. Many people, though, remain unconvinced by some of the explanations.

Reverting to the origin of life, the prevailing scientific theory seems to be that all life has its origin in one single event where some simple entity was lifeless at one moment but had the qualities of living and being able to reproduce itself the next. And the idea is that all life on earth then developed, through a series of mutations and natural selection, from that one common parent – the ultimate ancestor of every human being, every fish, every tree and so on. It is legitimate to question whether that idea is sustainable and whether, if life was created out of non-life at one point, it could happen again or even all the time. And if not, why not? And how did this wholly inanimate object in a wholly inanimate world suddenly change so that it was capable of feeding (albeit presumably in some incredibly simple way – there was, after all, no other living thing to eat) and reproducing?

My personal view is that there is a very strong case for arguing that life began on earth a few billion years ago and I do not therefore believe that the biblical account of creation is an accurate record of something that took place just a few thousand years ago. Others disagree but, in the end, I feel that the topic is not of primary interest for the Christian who wishes merely to acknowledge God as the originator of everything. For me, the miracles of creation lie in the fact of making something out of nothing, and in creating life out of no life, not in the mechanics of how these acts are done. There is nothing in this view that contradicts official Catholic teaching, by the way: see, for example, the heading of *Creation and Evolution* in the article *Creation* in the Catholic Encyclopaedia[41].

And we can go back a step further than the origins of life to seek answers to the origins of the universe itself. Imagine an observer who has, as it were, been contemplating nothingness for infinite time. After, say, a few trillion years of watching, the observer's eye is caught by a sudden movement: until a moment ago, there had been nothing, for ever, everywhere; now, suddenly, there is an explosion of matter. Science teaches us about cause and effect; physics operates according to laws that we can comprehend, but nowhere can science explain how everything is created out of nothing.

The scientific counter-argument is on the lines that Christians are merely pushing the boundaries one stage further back: if God created the universe, where did God come from? The difference is that Christians believe in a God who is outside the laws of physics, who in fact created those laws; a God whose perfect completeness is such that He just exists, without beginning or end. We do not claim to be able to get our heads round it, for it is indeed mind-blowing; the Christian view is to accept that we are incapable of grasping certain concepts or dimensions. And is it not ultimately more logical to argue for the existence of a God who is outside the laws of physics than to state that everything must be governed by the principles of cause and effect apart from the question of where the universe appeared from in the first place? And that is just when we try to explain *how* it all happened. Scientists cannot, of course, begin to address the other question: "why?".

So where should a thinking Christian stand on these issues? Evolution is a clever concept and there is much scientific evidence to support it, but it is not without its problems. The origin of matter itself also presents problems to the scientist. Ultimately, in the theological arena, the question of *how* life came about is perhaps unimportant. Christians who do not believe literally in the biblical stories of creation find that that takes nothing away from their faith at all. The Old Testament is a complete mixture of written accounts, including history (told from a specific viewpoint), literature, poetry and an attempt to set down an early but obviously incomplete understanding of God's nature. Christians believe scripture to be God-inspired and therefore believe that there is no part of the bible that can simply be ignored. But to insist on a literal interpretation strikes many as unjustified and unnecessary – how much richer and more valuable it is if we read Genesis (for example) not as an historic account but as a statement of God's infinitely creative power from which all life and everything in the universe stems.

But what about science more generally? Is it not the case that science can now explain pretty much everything away? No: I believe that it will be obvious from a reading of this booklet that there are still plenty of happenings for which science cannot account. And, though some would have us believe otherwise, there are plenty of scientists around who either believe or are at least open to the possibility that Christian belief is true.

A survey of doctors in the USA found that more than three quarters believed in God and 59 per cent believed in an after life[42]. A further report published in *The Guardian* in 2003[43] surveyed US scientists more generally and found that believers and non-believers were roughly equally balanced (40 per cent to 45 per cent, with the rest uncertain). Furthermore, and despite all the scientific developments of the twentieth century, the percentages had barely changed over an 80 year period. That report also referred to a number of high achiever scientists who publicly profess their Christian belief, including Colin Humphreys (a Cambridge professor of materials science, and a Baptist) and Tom McLeish (professor of polymer physics at Leeds). Reference is also made to Russell Stannard, emeritus professor of physics at the Open University. Asked if he was worried that science would explain away his belief, he replied:

> "No, because a starting point you can have is: why is there something rather than nothing? Why is there a world? Now I cannot see how science could ever provide an answer."

As it happens, the question of faith was also aired in *The Times* shortly before the first edition of this booklet went to print. The following extracts are both from letters printed on 7 October 2006:

> "Science cannot make a statement either way on the supernatural." – Andy McIntosh, Professor of Thermodynamics and Combustion Theory, University of Leeds.

"For some reason science seems to be in fear of faith and seeks to distance itself from its religious and philosophical manifestations. It trivialises them." Dr Mike Snow, former senior research scientist, Medical Research Council.

And there is one topic which could have had a chapter dedicated to it in this booklet, but which I have left out because it has not had any serious bearing on my own faith development. The topic in question is that of reports from those who have been clinically dead but who have been brought back to life on the operating table. On 5 October 2006, *The Times* contained an interview with Dr Peter Fenwick, former Fellow of the Institute of Psychiatry and head of the epilepsy unit at the Maudsley Hospital. Through his medical work, Dr Fenwick became convinced that human consciousness can survive death: "This isn't a belief system of mine, you know. I'm a scientist, totally data-driven". For his book *The Truth in the Light* he and his wife interviewed countless patients who had survived near death experiences. Given a severe mauling by the medical establishment, Dr Fenwick explained the reaction of his fellow scientists as "fear … and an inability to tolerate ambiguity".

+ + +

Chapter 10

~ Conclusion ~

So what can be made of it all?

Paradoxically, for the Christian, much of what is described in this booklet is rather unimportant. We can all be amazed or inspired at a miraculous healing when it occurs and we can perhaps find the story of Padre Pio or of Lourdes helpful at times when our faith wavers. But once we come off the fence and believe then we no longer need visible signs as a basis for faith. For the Catholic, a miracle greater than any healing or apparition occurs invisibly every time the Mass is said.

In the end, Christianity is about *faith*. God could make himself known to everyone in an unambiguous way but in his great wisdom has chosen not to do so. As Jesus said to the disciple Thomas, who had been absent when Jesus first appeared and who had initially refused to believe in the resurrection, "You believe because you can see me. Blessed are those who have not seen and yet believe" [44]. And yet we are given these signs, not to be the foundations on which our faith is built but as pointers to a different perspective in a complex world.

I believe that the observations recorded in this booklet are all reason-based and that they all revolve around individuals who acted in good faith. Furthermore, the fruits of everything described in these pages have been positive, in terms of spiritual growth for those who have witnessed or heard about the events.

If any reader is coming cold to all of this, and yet has struggled this far, I readily acknowledge that much of what is discussed in this booklet seems simply too far from our day to day perception of the world to be believable. I would just say to such a reader to use this booklet as a starting point and so to take at least one topic and approach it fairly and with an open mind. For this has been just the briefest and most simplistic introduction to some incredibly complex issues. Learn more fully about the happenings at Medjugorje, or do some serious research into the life of Padre Pio or read the book by Sister Briege McKenna. In the end, we must all form our own views of what we believe but I do not think that anyone looking into the lives of these people can seriously conclude that they are either fraudulent or self-deceiving.

And finally, a very brief word about suffering. I do not propose to go into any depth as it is beyond the remit of this booklet, but we cannot ignore the question altogether. Suffering is the most difficult issue for a Christian to explain; whatever explanations may be given, there never seems to be a convincing way of reconciling the existence of an all-powerful, all-loving God with the extent and variety of suffering that we see in the world. Faced with a mother whose child has just died, or with a child who is orphaned, or with anyone who is suffering extreme physical or emotional pain, there is no easy answer to this question. A few observations are all that I can offer:

- The Christian believes that suffering can be turned to some good. We believe, after all, in a man-God who willingly suffered and died so as to build a bridge across the gulf that had formed between a perfect God and a far from perfect mankind.

- Catholics, and some other Christians, take the view that individual sufferings can be offered up so as to participate willingly in that redemptive process.

- We can perhaps all sense that whilst suffering at an individual level seems inexplicable, the alternative Brave New World of a society with no suffering is not a place where we would wish to live.

- Despite all the seemingly inexplicable injustices at an individual level, we can perhaps accept that there is a link between free will and suffering: without the possibility of suffering, there could perhaps be no free will. If God were to intervene at every moment to prevent all suffering then the reality of human freedom would evaporate.

- If God exists, he must certainly be outside anything we can perceive of time and space. Sufferings that are unimaginable in this life will surely gain some sort of perspective if seen through the lens of eternity.

- Death, which we often perceive as the greatest of all suffering, is for the Christian merely the start of the big adventure. This is not to belittle the pain of death – Jesus himself wept when he heard that his friend Lazarus was dead – but the pain is in the dying and in the loss that is left behind for those who live on. Many a Christian will, in Dylan Thomas' words, "rage against the dying of the light", just as a non-believer will, but perhaps only because we cannot perceive what is to come.

- Finally, if we profess a belief in a good and loving God then we also have to acknowledge the existence of opposing forces of darkness, truly powerful and truly malevolent. Those dark forces often seem to have the upper hand for now but the Christian promise is that they will not ultimately prevail.

I cannot for one moment claim that this is a satisfactory response, for I don't pretend to have any easy answers to this issue. But suffering has to be put in the balance when deciding where we stand on the existence of God. If the weight of all the other factors tilts us in favour of belief then all we can do is to acknowledge that suffering is a part of the package, and is a part that most of us are not privileged to understand in this life. Those who feel able to do so can seek to turn the evil of their suffering to good spiritual use, and we all have an obligation to work hard to alleviate the suffering of others.

If the earlier pages of this booklet have inspired, but the problem of suffering remains a real stumbling block, readers could do much worse than to turn to the writings of C S Lewis, in particular *The Problem of Pain* and *A Grief Observed*.

In one of his interviews[45], Dawkins says simply that "there is just no evidence for the existence of God". At one level, the Christian would agree: we are asked to take Christianity on faith, rather than to seek scientific proof. At another level, though, this booklet has sought to demonstrate that there are numerous Christian phenomena that are not susceptible to any rational explanation. Furthermore, these accounts are just the tip of the iceberg – there are many other good and sane individuals, across the centuries and from all over the world, who have given extraordinary testimonies of their Christian experiences. If we look in the right places, and with an open mind, is it really fair to claim that "there is just no evidence"?

In the end, we have to jump one way or the other on the question of whether it is all true. The one view says, perhaps, that Jesus existed but was deluded by the superstitions of his age. His disciples, who had spent three complete years with him and had witnessed his death on the cross decided to devote the rest of their lives to their beliefs, and ultimately died for them; so they too were presumably taken in, even to the point of meeting the resurrected Jesus on numerous occasions. So too, many thousands of individuals in the early church were duped (or fooled themselves) into believing that something was worth living and dying for.

The reports of the miracles were either invented (by people who were prepared to die to sustain their inventions) or were somehow a big party trick that managed to convince huge crowds of followers; the trick was especially clever when it seemed to include within less than 72 hours the reappearance of a man who had been publicly tortured to death on a cross. Similarly, miracles that are reported today are purely illusions, even when they include huge numbers of cures of long-established physical diseases.

Several hundred people over the centuries have somehow created a pretence that they are suffering the wounds of Christ on their hands and feet, often maintaining that pretence for decades despite living extraordinarily holy and humble lives and being subjected to every type of test and trial. In some cases, they have done so despite being totally paralysed.

Bernadette at Lourdes was simply impressionable, despite the subsequent reports of medical cures on a wide scale. The three peasant children at Fatima were likewise taken in by some freak weather phenomenon that occurred on the same day each month for half a year and ended with a spectacular show on the predicted last day; or perhaps the three young shepherd children simply managed to stage a trick that fooled everyone and was reported in newspapers worldwide. In Medjugorje six children invented a lie and all six have sustained that lie throughout their adult lives, continuing to do so until this day, despite being harangued by the authorities and subjected to every conceivable testing technique.

Or perhaps it is all just true.

Chapter 11

~ Consequences ~

But if this Christianity really is true, is there not a high price to pay for signing up? In a way, this is the wrong question for it focuses not on the value but on the cost. If it is true, there is a sense in which nothing else will ever matter quite as much again. The price may be high but the 'product' (in commercial terms) is incomparably better than anything else on offer.

In the end, Christianity is simply about love. It tells us to give rather than to take, to look after others before ourselves, to exercise restraint rather than indulging ourselves in every way. And yet it contains a paradox in that it promises that we will be happier as a result, not just now but for eternity. It all seems incredibly counter-cultural for those of us living in the west in the twenty-first century.

Many others, including the present pope Benedict XVI, have written much wiser words about the Christian meaning of love than I ever could. In simple terms, though, the Christian is told to love God, acknowledging Him as creator, as provider of life itself, and as source of all that is good. And the Christian also has to love his neighbour, which can perhaps be thought of as a command to view and treat each other as fully human, as people rather than as objects to be used. In a way this is obvious but it is astonishing how far the implications can go and how difficult it can be in practice. Whether we think of money, sex, work, entertainment, the way we treat the very young or the very old, or indeed almost any field of human life, it is so easy to use one another as objects, to seek our own gain at the expense of someone else's humanity and dignity. Christianity says no. It may go against our natural instincts, and nobody gets it right all the time, but that is the calling.

+ + +

Notes, bibliography and further reading

1. See, for example:
    dir.salon.com/story/news/feature/2005/04/30/dawkins/
    index.html.
2. www.ewtn.com/library/ENCYC/JP2fides.htm
3. www.katapi.org.uk/4Gospels/Ch1.htm.
4. en.wikipedia.org/wiki/Gospel.
5. www.newadvent.org/cathen/06655b.htm.
6. www.newadvent.org/cathen/08377a.htm.
7. Tacitus, *Annals* 15.44, quoted at
    en.wikipedia.org/wiki/Great_Fire_of_Rome.
8. www.gutenberg.org/catalog/world/readfile?pageno=117&
    fk_files=2025.
9. Pliny, *Letters*, translated by William Melmoth, revised by
    W.M.L. Hutchinson (Cambridge: Harvard Univ. Press,
    1935), vol. II, X:96, cited in Habermas, *The Historical
    Jesus*, 199.
10. When referring to books of the bible, the name and
    chapter number are given by way of abbreviation. In this
    example, therefore, "Matthew 1" refers to the first chapter
    of Matthew's gospel.
11. For a complete list of biblical miracles, see:
    www.christiananswers.net/dictionary/miracle.html.
12. See, for example:
    www.catholic.net/rcc/Periodicals/Homiletic/May97/gospels
    .html.
13. See:
    www.westmont.edu/~fisk/Articles/TacitusAndPlinyOnThe
    EarlyChristians.html.
14. See:
    www.catholiceducation.org/articles/religion/re0021.html.
15. Luke 24:18. The passage is worth reading if only to enjoy
    the irony of the context in which the words are spoken.
16. See, for example: Mark 3:13 to 19.
17. See: www.newadvent.org/cathen/11744a.htm.
18. See:
    www.allaboutfollowingjesus.org/early-christian-
    persecution-faq.htm for a brief summary of how each is
    thought to have died.
19. *Miracles Do Happen*, by Briege McKenna and Henry
    Libersat. Published by Charis Books. ISBN 0892833165.

20. *The Happiest People on Earth*, by Demos Shakarian with John and Elizabeth Sherrill. Published by Hodder & Stoughton. ISBN 0340665114.
21. www.newadvent.org/cathen/09389b.htm.
22. en.wikipedia.org/wiki/Our_Lady_of_Fatima.
23. See, for example: www.ewtn.com/fatima/apparitions/October.htm.
24. www.medjugorje.org/faq.htm.
25. See: www.ewtn.com/Devotionals/mercy/dmmap.htm or www.catholicity.com/prayersdevotions/divinemercy.html.
26. www.catholicity.com/prayersdevotions/divinemercy.html
27. Acts 2:7.
28. 1 Corinthians 14:5
29. Galatians 6:17
30. www.livingmiracles.net/Stigmata.html
31. www.atheists.org/flash.line/vatican4.htm
32. en.wikipedia.org/wiki/Casa_Sollievo_della_Sofferenza
33. William M Carrigan – see www.padrepio.net/PioIntro.html
34. Once more, see www.livingmiracles.net/ Stigmata.html
35. *Stigmata and Modern Science* – Rev. Charles M Carty – Tan Books and Publishers, Inc.
36. www.ewtn.com/library/mary/mrobin.htm
37. www.christendom-awake.org/pages/cts/intromar.html
38. *The Origin of Species* – Chapter 4 – Charles Darwin.
39. *The Origin of Species* – Introduction – Charles Darwin.
40. *The Blind Watchmaker* – Chapter 1 – Richard Dawkins – Penguin: ISBN 0140144811.
41. www.newadvent.org/cathen/04470a.htm
42. www.estatevaults.com/bol/archives/001661.html
43. www.guardian.co.uk/life/feature/story/0,13026,1034872,00.html
44. John 20:29
45. See, again, dir.salon.com/story/news/feature/2005/04/30/dawkins/index.html